SENSES

TOUCH

Anita Ganeri

W
FRANKLIN WATTS
LONDON • SYDNEY

An Appleseed Editions book

First published in 2014 by Franklin Watts
338 Euston Road, London NW1 3BH

© 2012 Appleseed Editions

Created by Appleseed Editions Ltd,
Well House, Friars Hill, Guestling,
East Sussex TN35 4ET

Designed and illustrated by Guy Callaby
Edited by Mary-Jane Wilkins

A CIP record for this book is available from
the British Library

ISBN 978 1 445 31511

Dewey Classification: 612.8'8

Picture acknowledgements
l – left, r – right, c = centre, t = top, b = bottom
page 1 GekaSkr/Shutterstock; 2 iStockphoto/Thinkstock;
3t Hemera/Thinkstock; c iStockphoto/Thinkstock;
b wavebreakmedia ltd/Shutterstock; 4 mojito.mak.gmail.com/
Shutterstock; 6l Minerva Studio/Shutterstock; r iStockphoto/
Thinkstock; 7tr karam Miri/Shutterstock; tr Brand X Pictures/
Thinkstock; bl and br iStockphoto/Thinkstock; 8 MaszaS/
Shutterstock; 9t Photodisc/Thinkstock; b Hemera/Thinkstock;
10 iStockphoto/Thinkstock; 13 Hemera/Thinkstock;
14 iStockphoto/Thinkstock; 15 Hemera/Thinkstock;
16 Suzanne Tucker/Shutterstock; 17 Werner Heiber/
Shutterstock; 18 Photodisc/Thinkstock; 19 Stockbyte/
Thinkstock; 20 Dmitriy Shironosov/Shutterstock; 21t Hemera/
Thinkstock; 21 Hemera Technologies/Thinkstock; 22t PRILL
Mediendesign und Fotografie/Shutterstock; l Anton Prado
PHOTO/Shutterstock; r Milos Luzanin/Shutterstock;
b Jaroma/Shutterstock; 23t iStockphoto/Thinkstock;
b Aaron Amat/Shutterstock; image beneath folios holbox/
Shutterstock
Cover: iStockphoto/Thinkstock

Printed in China

Franklin Watts is a division of Hachette Children's Books,
an Hachette UK company
www.hachette.co.uk

Contents

Touchy, feely

What happens when you stroke a cat? What does it **feel** like?

Does the cat's fur feel soft and silky, or hard and rough?

Touch is one of your senses.
Your senses tell you about the
world around you.

Your five senses are:

sight

hearing

touch

taste

smell

You see with your eyes

You hear with your ears

You touch with your fingers

You taste with your tongue

You smell with your nose

What can you touch?

Your sense of touch tells you how things feel. You can feel whether things are rough or smooth.

You can feel whether something is hard or soft. You can feel whether something is hot or cold.

Your skin

You feel things with your **skin**. Your whole body is covered in stretchy skin.

8

Your skin can bend and stretch as much as you can.

Your skin holds your body together. It bends and stretches as you move about.

In most places, your skin is only as thick as **cardboard**.

Under your skin

Your skin has two layers. The top layer gets worn out, but new skin quickly grows again.

The skin on your hands has ridges to help you grip.

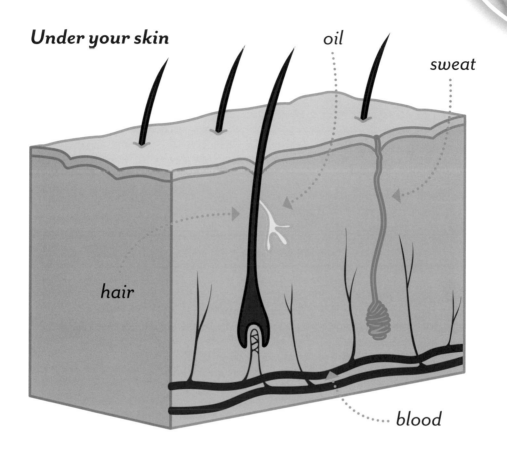

Under your skin

oil

sweat

hair

blood

Lots of things happen under your skin. Tiny tubes carry blood. Other parts make oil and sweat.

Touch messages

There are also millions of tiny **nerves** under your skin.
Each kind feels a different thing.

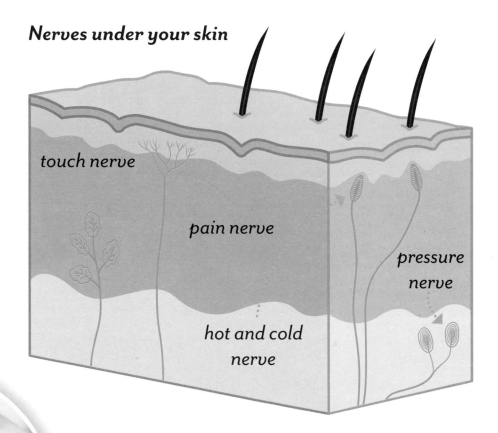

Nerves under your skin

touch nerve

pain nerve

hot and cold nerve

pressure nerve

Then the nerves send messages to your brain to tell you what you can touch and feel.

Sensitive skin

Some parts of your skin are more sensitive than others because they have more nerves.

The skin on your toes has lots of nerves in it.

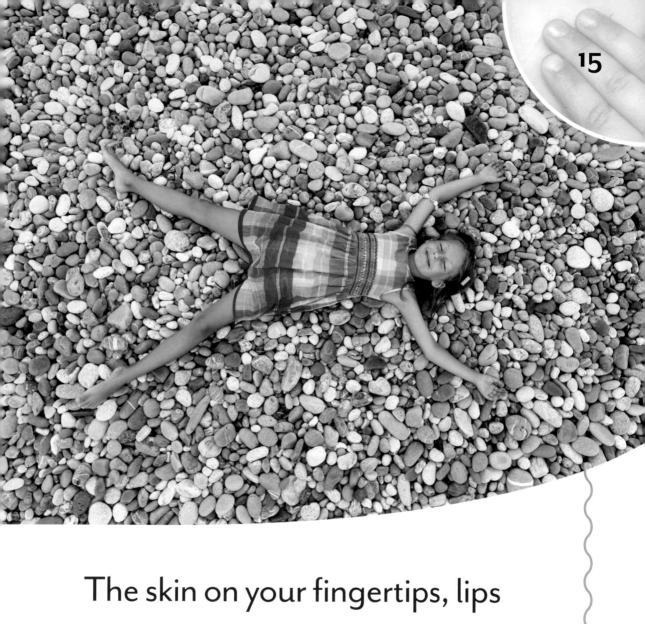

The skin on your fingertips, lips and toes is the most sensitive. The skin on your back and bottom is the toughest.

Painful touch

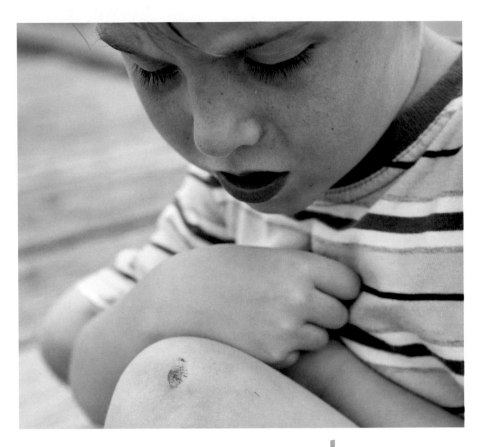

Grazing your knee can hurt a lot. But pain can be a very useful feeling, too.

The **pain** warns you that something is wrong so you can stop your body getting hurt more.

Useful skin

Your skin does lots of other useful jobs. It stops your insides getting harmed. It is also waterproof.

Your skin quickly
mends itself if
you cut yourself.
It makes a scab
until new skin grows.

Hair and nails

Hair grows out of tiny holes in your skin. Hair grows on your body and head.

What colour hair do you have?

You have about **five million hairs on** your body and head.

Nails also grow from your skin. They are useful if you have an itch!

Touch facts

The patterns on the skin on your fingertips are called your fingerprints. No one else has the same fingerprints as you.

The dust in your house is mostly made up of dead skin cells. You lose millions of these every day.